essence revisited

Slipping Past the Shadows of Illusion

Darryl Bailey

NON-DUALITY PRESS

Editor: Sandra Stuart

Layout: Link Phillips, Julian Noyce & John Gustard

www.non-dualitypress.com

ISBN: 978-0-9566432-6-1

In 2003, I self-published the book *Essence* with the help of two friends, Sandra Stuart and Link Phillips, acting as editor and layout designer. *Essence Revisited* is a refinement of that first offering. Much of the original text is retained; the main points are still here, in simpler fashion; some elements are gone for the sake of clarity, and new considerations have arisen; but it still carries the flavour of those many summer hours that the three of us gathered in Sandra's gazebo, excited by life's dance and the possibility of presenting it on a page.

Darryl Bailey
September 2010

For those who are drawn to it.

Introduction

The ideas offered here are not the only possible views of
existence.
If you relate to them,
wonderful;
if not,
wonderful.

Question and Answer: Part I

Q: *You describe the human race as being perfect as it is, as perfect as any other manifestation of nature. You also say we're not responsible for who we are or what we do. This is very different from other teachings, such as Buddhism, that promote practices for self-restraint, self-knowledge, self-improvement, and so on.*

DB: It seems so, at first. Students of spiritual teachings often believe those teachings are about perfecting themselves through great effort. They do various practices in the hope of turning themselves into something called an enlightened being.

They assume an enlightened being is someone who never experiences unpleasant emotions, like confusion, anger, sorrow, jealousy, fear, depression, and so on.

The students are hoping to escape these difficulties and attempt to make themselves calm and contented all the time. They're looking for some kind of understanding and skill that will give them control over the unpleasant aspects of life.

I meet them after they've been doing their self-development practices for many years and they're wondering why those practices haven't worked, why they don't feel perfected, and why they still experience unpleasant emotions.

It's because the so-called enlightenment that these traditions offer has nothing to do with self-improvement or control.

You can practice observing your thoughts and emotions, analyzing them, restraining them, and attempting to overcome them as much as you want, but there's a basic delusion in that situation that never gets addressed and that delusion is what these teachings are ultimately about.

All the great spiritual teachings ultimately point to a freedom that has nothing to do with self-improvement or control.

Q: *And that freedom is?*

DB: The realization that life isn't our doing; we're a movement of nature. Everything, just as it is in any moment, is the already complete and pure expression of existence; it's never been a person accomplishing anything.

Q: *Could you elaborate on that?*

DB: Yes. If we examine life, we can observe that everything is changing. Even the most stable looking "thing" in existence is undergoing some change in each moment.

This is easy to see in things that change quickly, such as thoughts, moods, and emotions, but it's not so immediately obvious in things that change slowly, such as walls, furniture, and mountains. However, if we take the time to seriously consider it, we can acknowledge the fact that everything is changing.

If it isn't maintained, this house we're sitting in will eventually dry up, turn to dust, and blow away. Nobody has the impression that it will stay brand-new for hundreds of years and then grow old overnight. Instead, there is the sense that it's ageing slowly and that it's changing right now, in subtle ways.

If we look at trees that have fallen in a forest, it's easy to observe that they're decomposing. They're slowly vanishing, turning to powder, and those bits of powder will eventually become so small they'll seem to disappear. The form of a tree is actually a movement that unfolds from a seed, grows to maturity, and eventually fades away.

It's the same with everything in existence. The Himalayan mountains are growing one inch every year, while other mountain ranges are grinding down and will eventually be flat land. There once was an ocean in this place where we're sitting, but it's not here now, and what is is changing in its own ways.

The planet earth began as hot gases that became molten lava and then solid rock, and this rock will move through its various appearances until it eventually disappears. Astronomers watch entire galaxies blipping out of existence in the far reaches of the universe.

If we explore life, with its plants growing, creatures ageing, rivers flowing, cities transforming, climates fluctuating, continents shifting, and so on, we find constant movement. If we look to our own being, we find the same happening: breath coming and going, heart beating, thoughts flowing, moods shifting, perceptions altering, sounds dancing, twinges, pains, pulsations, vibrations, and so on.

All of existence is a moving, vibrant event.

It doesn't matter what it is — an atom, a thought, a sound, a situation, a body, a mental state, a plant, a storm, a mountain, or a galaxy — everything that we know of is changing, either quickly or slowly. Inward and outward, big or small, there is only this shift and flux. If this is fully acknowledged, it may be realized that this is all that actually exists.

No object or "thing" is ever truly formed anywhere. Nothing is ever established or defined. No thing ever comes to stay, to exist, to "be".

What we usually consider to be a collection of things, the many things of the universe, is more accurately pointed to as a "great spirit", since this reflects the fact that it is a vital, flowing event.

In some spiritual traditions it's referred to as an unformed presence, or simply "un-form", since constant change is the ongoing absence of any particular arrangement or shape.

This constant flow isn't some imaginary situation: it's all that is ever experienced. It's everything we are and everything around us. Inward and outward, there is only an unformed liveliness.

Some call it energy, quantum energy, or dark energy; some call it pure consciousness or pure awareness; some call it Mind, with a capital m; some refer to it as the ever-shifting ocean of existence; and some simply give it labels like God, Tao, or Atman.

Obviously, a happening or presence that always changes can't be described as anything in particular. It's an ever-shifting dynamic. Completely acknowledging this vital event brings a major shift in the sense of living.

If existence is seen as a collection of things, there is

the hope of finding and holding some "thing" that won't change. There's also the belief that existence can be described and understood. But this perspective brings a great deal of unhappiness, because it constantly refuses the dance that life is.

We want life to be something in particular — something pleasant, something definable, something stable and secure — a particular way of being. But existence isn't anything in particular. There is only an ever-shifting event, the absence of any intrinsic form.

The belief in form constantly struggles with the movement of existence and that movement will always break through any false impression of stability, leaving feelings of frustration, confusion, and sorrow.

If, however, it's realized that every so-called thing, including you, is actually motion, there is no expectation of stability; there's never any form to hold or to understand. There is simply a magical dance of ever-changing appearances.

If we ask the body to stop growing old, it does not. If we ask it to change only in healthy directions, it does

7

not. Even with our best efforts the body will, at some point, exhibit sickness, ageing, and death.

Ask your circumstances to stop changing, or to change only in pleasant directions, and they don't. The same is true for your various thoughts, feelings, perceptions, mental activities, states of mind, and all other apparent things.

Waves rise up and fade away. The breath inhales and exhales. The heart clenches and relaxes. There is the alternating appearance of sound/silence, light/dark, hot/cold, joy/sorrow, clarity/confusion, the pleasant and the unpleasant.

Whether it's the change of moods, viewpoints, bodies, the weather, the environment, and so on, life is an ever-shifting flow. No one is making this happen and no one can stop it.

We can try to stop it, to control thoughts, emotions, health, and so on, only to discover that the effects of such efforts are both limited and short-lived. No matter how much you've tried to make your life constantly pleasant, it hasn't worked.

For everyone, life is an ongoing dance of ups and downs. Realizing this allows us to see that, along with pleasant periods, there will be unpleasant periods. Difficulties arise, sometimes extreme, because this is the natural rhythm of existence expressing itself.

On one hand, this is a wonderful fact to learn. It dissolves a great deal of useless struggle and confusion when we simply acknowledge this obvious rhythm. However, most of us are then left with the feeling of being someone subject to the cold, cruel whims of existence, someone standing separate from the event, being abused by it. So let's look at this more closely.

If you sit, or lie down, and make no effort at all, you may discover another fact: everything happens on its own.

Breathing occurs without anyone doing it. The heart beats in the same way. Seeing occurs without anyone having to manipulate the rods and cones of the eye. Hearing, touching, tasting, smelling, and thinking simply happen. Feelings, thoughts, and moods come and go. Focuses of attention dance around; blood circulates; hair grows; the nervous system operates; and so on.

All of this simply happens. There isn't anyone doing it.

As a fertilized egg in the womb, we didn't decide to grow larger or decide to take a trip down the birth canal. Outside the womb, we didn't decide to begin growing, thinking, walking, or talking. No "self" directs any of this; it simply occurs as the compulsive flow of nature.

We don't create our bodies and we don't create our brains. We don't create the physical abilities, mental abilities, and lack of abilities, we are. We don't create the apparent needs, interests, and concerns that arise in any moment. All of this simply happens on its own.

We can't arbitrarily decide to be something else, to be a different body and brain, a different set of physical and mental abilities, different needs, interests, and concerns. Even if it appears as though we make decisions, they grow out of the needs, interests, and concerns that arise in any particular moment and there's no "self" that makes it happen.

Nature presents situations that demand a decision and the response to those situations is a movement of the only body, need, interest, and ability that nature also presents.

We don't *have* this body, need, interest, and ability; we *are* this body, need, interest, and ability. Again, if you sit and make no effort, the movement that you are expresses itself quite clearly — the dance of pulsations, vibrations, thoughts, moods, needs, interests, and so on — but there's never an experience of anything owning that movement.

Some incline toward art, some to science, others to social service, to family, to business, religion, technology, and so on. If your main love is art, you can't arbitrarily decide to love science instead.

Everyone's experience indicates that everything we are, and everything we do, is simply the movement of existence itself. It's here that we come to the highest realization indicated in all the great spiritual traditions: we do not exist as anything apart from the flow of nature and that flow is an unformed, inexplicable dance accomplishing itself.

Q: *You're saying we have no free will.*

DB: No, I'm saying be very careful with descriptions of existence; they contain a great deal of confusion and fear. If everything is acknowledged as it actually is, ever-shifting and unformed, it's an indefinable happening. All that's ever experienced is an unformed dance presenting itself. It's the vibrant, pulsing, luminous event that this moment is. There is only that.

Q: *But surely that can't be the case. I mean, I've decided to come here and ask these questions and you've decided to answer them the way you do. That's free will.*

DB: Yes, but the decision you apparently made grows out of an interest in spiritual inquiry, out of the apparent interest, understanding, and need, that you are right now.

You didn't decide at some point in your life to be this interest, understanding, and need; it simply happens as a movement of nature. Someone else is out surfing, or studying international banking, while you're here asking me these questions. There's nothing you can do about it; you have to be the expression you are in this moment.

I also have an interest in spiritual inquiry, an interest I didn't create and can't ignore. If you come to me seriously investigating this matter, I'm compelled to respond to your questions.

I don't decide what my response will be. I'm capable of responding in only one way, and that response is what nature presents in this moment. I can't arbitrarily choose to be something else.

Q: *So, for you it's automatic; everything happens automatically.*

DB: Yes. You could also say spontaneously, organically.

Just as the ripples, bubbles, and waves of an ocean are not separate objects directing their lives — they're one movement — the various things in the universe are not separate objects directing their lives. They're also one movement.

All forms are motion. Form, or "thingness", is an illusion, and there's no cure for that illusion other than seeing that it's unreal.

Just as a rope, if it's not seen clearly, can seem to
be a snake, or a mirage can seem to be water, the
totally unformed, inexplicable dance of this moment
can seem to be people in a world. But that's a false
appearance.

Q: *And you're saying this is enlightenment.*

DB: Yes, realizing this is called enlightenment, but it's
the realization of a happening that can't be defined
in any way at all. This happening can have no true
description, not even the description of a person
getting enlightened.

There's simply the unformed, luminous, pulsing
dance that this moment is. It magically appears to be
all kinds of things, but those appearances are false.
None of them are a stable form: there is only constant
movement, and there's no possible explanation for it.

Q: *It's a pure knowing.*

DB: No, that's another fantasy.

Q: *But what's knowing that?*

DB: Nothing. "Knowing" is a meaningless label.

Consider this: with a newborn, there are no labels for existence — there is no storyline — no "knower", no "knowing" and no "object of knowing.". There's the same basic warming, cooling, sounding, silencing, lightening, darkening, tingling, trembling, event that this moment is, but there are no labels for it. It's a totally mysterious happening.

If I point to something nearby, this for example, and I ask you what this is, you would give me a sound, the sound "chair", but that sound is not what I'm pointing to.

If I ask a newborn what this is, the child isn't going to say "chair". The child doesn't have a sound or symbol for anything. There's simply a mysterious happening without labels. For the so-called child there isn't even a question; it's just meaningless "blah, blah, blah".

At some point, labels will arise as part of this happening, but sounds like "chair" and "knowing" and "child" have no more meaning than sounds like "dizzlydonk" and "wotafaroo".

Existence is a totally mysterious event in its arising and, no matter how many sounds and labels appear in this happening, it remains a totally mysterious event. Just as the barking of a trained seal is not explaining existence, no matter how many sounds we're trained to bark, we're also not explaining existence.

Q: *So, how is this felt to be freedom?*

DB: In any moment, there is only an unformed, inexplicable happening moving on its own, but there's the strange belief that it's a "self" — living in — and "knowing" — a world of "things". It's an absolutely mysterious event, however; there's the apparent delusion that it's being understood and the further delusion that there's something intrinsically wrong with it.

There's a desperate attachment to the story of a me that is knowing and directing something called life, and the feeling that I'm not doing it correctly, because it's never what it "should" be. There's a general feeling of guilt for our perceived flaws and shortcomings, and the judging of everyone else as being even more flawed, in order to feel better about the situation.

As a result, there's an aching urge to correct ourselves, and everything else, and a huge amount of frustration and sorrow at the fact that it never seems to get corrected.

But all of this is an extraordinary fantasy. Existence, as it's experienced, is a totally inexplicable happening presenting itself. There can't be anything wrong with it. Realizing this brings an incredible sense of relief and rest.

Q: *Nothing wrong? All over the world we have starvation, wars, brutalities. How can you say there's nothing wrong?*

DB: These are the natural expressions of existence. Look at any forest environment, or ocean environment, and you'll find the same apparent hardship and cruelty. The difficulty with this is the strange assumption that we somehow exist outside the movement of nature and that we're in charge of it.

The idea that we're in charge of existence is a delusion. Everything we are is an expression of nature. We're not holding existence together with our efforts; our efforts themselves are the movement of nature.

We obviously don't create our physical and mental abilities, our bodies, needs, interests, urges, understandings, and concerns, therefore; we don't create our actions, or anything else.

Q: *That doesn't seem very liberating, to discover I'm a total slave.*

DB: That's not what I'm saying. There is no you that stands separate from existence. You're not being pushed around by it. Everything you appear to be, and all that you appear to do, is not a definable you at all; it's the unformed, inexplicable dance of the universe.

You're expressed in the same way the stars in the night sky are expressed, or any other appearance of nature is expressed. How can there be anything wrong with you? Which snowflake is doing it wrong? Which squirrel is making a mistake in its squirreling? What storm is making a bad life decision?

In any moment, everything is the only possible expression it can be. Seeing this doesn't make everything pain-free or flow in a pleasant way. It simply acknowledges that, in any moment, life is whatever it is, and it's not personal.

Einstein pointed out that we're part of the movement of existence and are no more responsible for our actions than an inanimate object, such as a stone, is responsible for its behaviour.

The Upanishads declare that when everything is seen to be a movement of the Lord, the big Self — the great dance of existence — "you" are liberated. There is no you apart from the dance.

The Buddha declared, *"What is is unformed; descriptions don't apply, and realizing this puts an end to any belief in stories of 'me' and 'mine,' my existence, my doing."*

The Bible has God, the great Spirit, declaring, *"I am the I am (the basic happening, the amness, the isness). I create light, darkness, peace, and evil; I do all of it."*

In all cases, there's an indefinable event, or presence, appearing to be many things, but those appearances are false. The stories of you and me, of various forms, of one thing influencing another, and so on, are a fantasy.

Q: *But if you convince us that we're not responsible for our actions it could lead to chaos. Without a sense of responsibility, we could do terrible things or give up doing altogether.*

DB: When the mind first hears these ideas it may attempt to reject them out of an irrational fear. It throws forth many objections, such as the ones you just mentioned. Or it will worry about being a mindless robot. If we're functioning to the laws of nature, doesn't that mean we're merely robots? It brings fears of determinism and fatalism.

There's the fantasy that we'll be trapped in some fixed mechanical way of behaving, with no hope of improving our situation, and we'll eventually sit around thinking, *"What's the use in doing anything?"*

This is the power of illusion, the irrational fear of an ego losing control, when all the while there hasn't been an ego in control. Acknowledging the vibrant flow of existence doesn't lead to some apathetic feeling of futility. Instead, it gives rise to the wonder and amazement of a magical presentation.

Seeing that we're the dance of the cosmos doesn't allow disorder, nor does it make us irresponsible. Even if a planet could know that it's an expression of the universe, it wouldn't be able to leave its orbit; the orbit is part of the expression. It's the same with us.

A sense of responsibility isn't your creation; it's an expression of nature. Love isn't your creation; it's also an expression of nature. Thinking isn't your creation. If existence didn't present it, it wouldn't exist.

Try giving up all that makes sense to you and all that you value. Try giving up the needs, interests, and concerns that you are in this moment. You can't do it, because you don't exist as anything apart from what's being presented.

Try doing nothing at all; just try it, and you'll eventually do something. You need to eat, sleep, go to the toilet, make a living, associate with friends. Everything you are is this compulsory movement. Even the urge to sit and rest is a spontaneous, compulsory action.

Whether you appear to be the boss of a big corporation, or a nun meditating in a cave, or anything else for that matter, isn't very important, because all of it is a totally inexplicable event accomplishing itself.

If you aren't already doing terrible things, realizing this isn't going to leave you with a new tendency to do them. Your so-called personality isn't your creation. Some people do terrible things, but, on any given day, most do not. The human race didn't decide it would be this way; it simply is this way.

This isn't some robotic existence. You're not being pushed around, or programmed, by something else; there is only the wild fullness of existence freely expressing itself. You don't exist as anything apart from that fullness.

In its illusions of form, this happening is endlessly creative. No two appearances of form are ever the same. Each and every instant is unique. No two identical things have ever been found. No two snowflakes, no two leaves, no two trees, no two moments.

This shifting, vibrant event is ultimately unpredictable, because it never repeats itself exactly. Some general predictions can be made, but the particulars are always a surprise. Even the generalities can be totally unexpected; just look at weather predictions.

Q: *So life is moving out of control.*

DB: Ideas of control don't apply to this; there is only movement. This flow has an inherent order, or current. Some call it an innate intelligence. A plant grows to that order. It twists this way and that, but eventually presents itself as a recognizable plant, even though it's never identical to any other.

The plant doesn't need control; it isn't consciously deciding to express itself this way. It doesn't hold itself together with efforts, nor does it decide the direction of its movement. No one has the impression that a plant is in charge of its growing; it's a movement of nature. Why would you think it's different for us?

Q: *How did your sense of this occur?*

DB: It's just happening. I could tell you a life story describing certain key moments, but all of that would be a fantasy; existence has no form or explanation.

Q: *But you have thoughts and stories.*

DB: No, not exactly; the movement that we call thoughts and stories is still happening, but it's a

23

totally indefinable event that simply presents itself.

As an infant, there is no understanding of anything; existence is an inexplicable buzz and tingle. It still is. It doesn't matter how many forms seem to exist, or how many apparent sounds arise and fade, all of it is an inexplicable, unformed dance presenting itself.

Q: *That doesn't help me understand this.*

DB: There is no understanding.

Q: *But can't you say more about this process of awakening?*

DB: Yes, if you want me to.

Q: *How did this happen to you?*

DB: It seemed to occur over a lifetime, with particular realizations coming in particular moments.

From an early age onward, there were periods when everything felt like one big happening. In my apparent twenties, I had difficulty understanding how anyone could be "making" decisions, since those decisions automatically arise from interests and abilities that none of us create.

Years later, I read a book stating that no one has ever had any experience of directing life. As I considered that statement, it was obviously true. The happenings that we call bodies, needs, interests, urges, and actions simply happen as a movement of nature.

At first, there was fear and confusion around all of this, because it seemed as though "I" was losing control; the storyline about a me being in control was threatened, but, as it became even more obvious that everything was happening on its own, the fear and confusion dissipated.

At a further point, it became obvious that existence is absolutely indefinable. Identifying forms doesn't explain anything, because existence has no form; everything is changing. The stories describing form can't possibly be the truth. Even stories about a me growing up, reading a book, and having realizations can't be true.

There's such a fascination with the appearance of existence, an attachment to how it looks, feels, and sounds, but existence has no particular look, feel, or sound.

Whatever it appears to be now is already on its way to some other appearance. Feelings are changing, moods are changing, thoughts are changing, sights are changing, sounds are changing, bodies are changing, activities are changing — cities, countries, planets, galaxies — all of this is happening on its own.

It's an inexplicable, vibrant dance without form. No one is making it happen, and no one can stop it.

Q: *What about spiritual practices for awakening?*

DB: Most so-called spiritual practices are the attempt to develop and control something. They're based on the fantasy that you're in charge of existence.

Those practices can't move beyond the story that you're in control, because they are the story that you're in control, the belief that you're going to make something happen by practising.

Moving beyond this belief can only occur by realizing what's actually happening, by realizing there is only

an indefinable, vibrant event accomplishing itself.
If you sit down and make no effort to do anything
at all, the basic nature of life expresses itself clearly.
This is the most profound meditation of any spiritual
tradition.

Some say it's a practice, but many would argue that
it's not a practice, because you're not doing anything.
In the Advaita community it's known as *satsang*; it
means association with being.

This doesn't mean we always have to sit around
doing nothing, but it's only when we're obviously
doing nothing that it becomes obvious everything is
presenting itself.

All the great spiritual teachings ultimately point
to this, no matter what else they seem to offer.
Whether it's called meditation, satsang, non-doing,
bare awareness, silent prayer, faith, the corpse pose,
just sitting, resting with the moment, and so on, isn't
important. In all cases, you're invited to make no
effort at all, and life may reveal itself to be the magical
event that it actually is.

The belief in form and personal doing may fade

away, and the vibrant, indefinable happening that everything is becomes obvious. In certain traditions, they say there is only God or Atman, but these are simply labels for the inexplicable liveliness that existence is. Call it whatever you have to; that's part of the dance.

There are teachings that say it will take thirty years of effort to realize this and others that invite you to it immediately, but they all have this in common. Whether it seems to occur after thirty years of effort, or seems to occur while hearing someone talk about it, or seems to occur by sheer accident, doesn't really matter. In all cases, it's the realization that everything is unformed, indefinable, and simply presenting itself.

If this realization occurs, all the descriptions and storylines are realized to be false. Thirty years of effort will be seen as fantasy. Stages of development will be seen as fantasy. Enlightenment will be seen as fantasy. These descriptions are false. There has never been anyone doing anything or arriving anywhere. In any so-called moment, there is only a totally unformed, inexplicable happening.

However, the illusion of an ego directing its life is so widespread that the urge to control is found almost everywhere. Even in spiritual circles there's a general assumption that the teaching must be about controlling something. There's usually an attempt to control and create perfect health, perfect calm, perfect love, perfect concentration, perfect understanding, and so on, according to some idealized fantasy. But this misses the essential point.

Q: *Which is?*

DB: Realization. As Alan Watts used to say, *"It's not true that you came into this world; you came out of it, like a flower comes out of a plant. You're something the whole universe is doing."*

Q: *But you've been meditating since you were fourteen years old. Surely that effort has created the understanding you have now.*

DB: With all due respect, that statement doesn't make any sense. When you say one thing causes another, you're actually saying there is only the movement of the universe. That's what the story of cause and effect ultimately states.

If we say meditating caused this understanding, it then has to be asked, what caused the meditating? We might say that it was based on the personality, ability, and need that I am. But what caused those things? We could say my genetic makeup had something to do with it, as well as my upbringing.

But what was the cause of those things? We then have to consider my parents, their genetics, their upbringing — my grandparents, great grandparents, and so on — back through the entire history of the human race.

However, everything that occurs in the cosmos supports the human race, so we have to look at that causal chain as well. Human beings exist on this planet with the help of oxygen, moisture, warmth, and light. Those conditions exist because of the movement of the galaxy, and the galaxy exists because the entire universe arranges itself as it does.

By acknowledging the entire movement of cause and effect, we come to the full happening of the universe and then run out of causes, because nothing else is evident.

If you really believe in the chain of cause and effect, you can't possibly believe there's a separate self accomplishing anything. Every atom of your being — everything you appear to think, say, and do — is an expression of the chain.

Q: *The point I wanted to make is that people do spiritual practices and get enlightened.*

DB: Yes, apparently so, but obviously this has nothing to do with the practices, since out of the hundreds of thousands of people apparently doing them, over the centuries, only a relatively small number have awakened.

Added to this is the fact that people who don't do spiritual practices also awaken. Einstein was a good example; Spinoza was another. They merely acknowledged their scientific observations.

I've heard of someone who was simply walking cattle back to a barn when he realized everything is the movement of nature. Another was having sex in a brothel. Another was sick, and spitting up blood, when this realization spontaneously occurred.

A young girl in Japan was dying and realized the mysterious movement that everything is. A boy in India simply stopped feeling that he was a particular person and, from that moment on, acknowledged the totally inexplicable event of existence.

Buddhist scriptures record that many people awoke while simply listening to the Buddha's talks. Advaita traditions are filled with similar stories involving other teachers.

This so-called enlightenment has presented itself in almost every situation you can imagine, yet there's no particular approach, no method, and no technique that is guaranteed to make it happen.

I'm not saying don't do spiritual practices and I'm not saying do them. I'm saying you don't have to concern yourself with that, because everything is a movement of nature. That includes the way you live, as well as any so-called awakening.

All that anyone can ever do is be the body, need, interest, urge, and action that nature is presenting in any particular moment.

Q: *Can anyone be enlightened?*

DB: Actually, no one can be enlightened. The so-called awakening is the realization that everything is absolutely indefinable; even the description of someone getting enlightened can't be true. Fixating on stories of enlightenment misses the miracle of life's full event.

If we walk into a forest, we marvel at the range and texture of nature's appearance. Each aspect of it is a wondrous expression of the universe — each tree, flower, blade of grass, bird, and butterfly. We don't feel any of it is a mistake.

We don't run up to the gnarled trees and tell them they should be like the tall, straight trees. We don't tell them that they're not trying hard enough, or they're not good enough, or they're not practising enough. We don't tell them they've gone in the wrong direction or that they should be something else. That would be ridiculous.

Instead, there's an appreciation of nature's manifestations, a wonder and delight. There's the feeling that each apparent thing is a movement of the whole and each is playing its part in the great event we call existence.

But go to the supermarket and see how much wonder and delight you find in the line of people at the checkout stand. In that situation, are we marvelling at the wondrous expressions of nature, or do we endlessly criticize nature's creation? *"Look at him behaving that way — what an idiot! And look at her; she shouldn't be dressed like that — she's too old!"*

We do the same at home, staring into the bathroom mirror, thinking, *"What's wrong with me? I shouldn't be like this. I should be something else, or something more."* Maybe we wish we were enlightened, or that everyone was enlightened, thinking it would make everything so much better.

But the enlightenment mentioned in the great spiritual traditions isn't a movement to a better existence. Instead, it's the realization that everything has to be exactly whatever it is in any particular moment. All of it is the already complete and pure expression of the cosmos.

Q: *So enlightenment can't save the world.*

DB: Save it from what? Every apparent thing is moving to its essential nature. No aspect of existence is doing it wrong, any more than any raindrop is doing it wrong. Just because it often seems unpleasant doesn't mean there's something wrong with it.

Existence is doing fine; in fact, it's doing us. Realizing this dissolves the self-righteous arrogance we usually exhibit. No one can take credit or blame for their behaviour. No one can give credit or blame to another.

Everything has to function in the way it functions. You have to be the body, need, interest, urge, and action that presents itself in this moment, and whatever it appears to be now is already on its way to some other expression.

It's a fantasy to think that your personal effort is responsible for what you are. There is no personal effort; nature gives rise to all apparent abilities, interests, and actions. To think there's a you that deserves the credit or blame is like thinking a flower deserves the credit or blame for the way it looks and behaves.

You can't make a mistake in living life, because whatever you appear to think, say, and do is simply the inexplicable dance of existence.

Q: *But we should consider life carefully before making decisions.*

DB: Logical thinkers think so. Intuitives do not.

Q: *Your point is?*

DB: No two expressions are ever the same. We can't become a copy of someone else.

As it states in the old children's story, a swan will feel ugly and out of place if it's trying to be a duck. It's also true that a duck will have difficulty in trying to be a swan.

Spiritual teachings encourage an appreciation of the amazingly unique and wondrous expression that each of us is. We're not trying to make ducks into swans. There's nothing wrong with ducks. There's nothing wrong with anything.

Q: *So, if a poisonous snake tries to bite me, I shouldn't do anything, because that's the natural expression of existence and there's nothing wrong with it.*

DB: That's not what I said. Even though there's nothing wrong in their expression, certain snakes, and certain people, are naturally considered to be dangerous, and we respond to danger automatically.

Nature is automatically expressing all apparent circumstances and all apparent responses to circumstance; it's one movement. Even if you try to suppress your natural responses, they'll eventually break through, because we don't exist as anything apart from that.

Q: *Okay, but after hearing all of this, I'm still puzzled as to how I'm supposed to live life.*

DB: Yes, most of us want someone to tell us how to live, but no one can tell us what we're supposed to be, or do. Each of us is a unique expression.

People go to spiritual teachers hoping to find something to make their lives constantly pleasant; they want control. They ask all kinds of questions, but it's really one basic question, *"How can I get enough understanding and control so that I never feel confused, frightened, sad, uncomfortable, and so on?"*

The answer to this is, *"You can't."*

The great spiritual teachings don't offer an escape from life's expressions. They offer the possibility of dispelling certain confusions, but not by gaining control over them; it's by acknowledging certain facts, such as the fact that every apparent thing is changing.

By acknowledging the actual happening of the moment, unrealistic ideas and expectations may fade away, along with the misery that accompanies them. The mistaken belief in ideas of form and personal doing may end, along with the confusions, anxieties, and frustrations that belief contains.

Life has an inherent sense of well-being, a natural richness and fullness. As a child, you didn't have to try to make yourself happy: life was a magical event, even though it was sometimes difficult and unpleasant. The focus was on the fullness of the event and not strongly attached to ideas of form and control.

Spiritual teachings are an invitation to once again acknowledge the great, unformed, vibrant event that life actually is, along with its inherent sense of magic and well-being.

You may appear to explore many teachings, both Eastern and Western, but your particular way of living will be unique. Just like any other expression of nature, you can never match another exactly.

You don't need to figure out what to do next; you don't have to worry about getting it right or wrong. The next priority, the next need, interest, and concern that you are, rises up on its own; it always has. As an apparent four year old, it was what it was; at ten, it was different; as a teenager, it was something else. In this moment, it's whatever it is, and it's automatically on its way to some other expression.

At times, it may seem vague and uncertain, but that's also the natural expression of existence.

There's no particular you to be found: there's simply the body, need, interest, urge, and action that nature is presenting in this moment and it's already on its way to something else. Before lunch, it was someone needing lunch; after lunch, it's different. Before bed, it's someone needing sleep; in the morning, it's different.

Maybe there's some major issue presenting itself,

and the responses to that issue are also presenting themselves. This may dance around in various ways for an apparently long period of time, but it will eventually move on to some radically different expression. There is only this unformed dance.

In realizing this, there's a growing trust in being the movement we are, a sense of wonder at the magical appearance of everything, and a sense of richness in the full and vital expression of the moment. There's also a tremendous sense of rest, because we don't have to hold ourselves together. Everything we appear to think, say, and do, in any particular moment, is automatically presenting itself.

As Jiddu Krishnamurti used to say, "*Perfection is this movement. We never seem to learn about this, that it is one movement.*"

Q: *Are you trying to get everyone to understand this?*

DB: Not at all. Only a certain percentage of the human population will have an interest in this. Others are expressed differently. There's nothing anyone can do about that, because there isn't anyone doing anything; there never has been.

Reflections I

The perspective presented here is not the only possible view of existence and it's important only to those who relate to it; it has no importance outside of that.

The coming together of people around a certain perspective has no more significance, or meaning, than robins gathering with robins and crows with crows. Like clouds gathering in the sky, it's the inexplicable play of existence doing what it does.

It's difficult for most people to consider that someone like Hitler is a perfectly natural expression of existence.

We accept the fact that sharks and tigers don't normally attack people, but some do. They're not the norm, but they are a harsh fact of life. Yet we find it so difficult to acknowledge that human beings are also expressed in this way.

Saints and sinners are both valid expressions of existence, just as kittens and scorpions are. It's a misconceived arrogance that condemns one over the other; both must be whatever they are.

One may appear gentle and passive, while the other is nasty and aggressive; in this they're different. But each is simply an indefinable expression of existence; in this they're equal.

This would be a doctrine of determinism if we existed as something separate from the movement of the universe, something being pushed around by it. But we're not separate from it; we are this movement.

This is what's meant when a tradition speaks of reaching the unconditioned. Life's mysterious event is not conditioned by anything, because it's an inexplicable, formless dynamic that is freely expressing itself. Nothing else is evident.

What is usually believed to be our conditioned personal behaviour is actually the inexplicable wholeness of existence freely expressing itself. Realizing this is what's meant by "reaching the unconditioned".

The ideas offered here may seem strange, but others who have expressed a similar view include Albert Einstein, Simone Weil, Nietzsche, Spinoza, Emerson, Thoreau, Goethe, Hafiz, Schopenhauer, Martin Luther, Teresa of Ávila, Juliana of Norwich, Saint Augustine, Thomas Hobbes, David Hume, Alan Watts, Immanuel Kant, Voltaire, David Bohm, the Zen masters, Sufi masters, Advaita sages, and the enlightened teachers of the Upanishads.

People want to awaken in order to make their worldly lives easier. What's revealed is that nothing needs transforming; every apparent thing, in any apparent moment, is already flowing to its true nature.

Any attempt to conform to some generalized standard of behaviour is suffering. Having general standards for human beings creates conflict with the fact that nature constantly gives rise to unique expressions that will never match another exactly.

To attempt to deny the unique manifestation you are is to suffer. You must be whatever you are in any apparent moment and, no matter what it appears to be now, it's unavoidably on its way to some other expression.

The mental agonies of life are wrapped around the idea that we're something separate from the movement of existence, a "me" owning and directing the thoughts, feelings, interests, urges, and actions.

The karmic chain of personal responsibility is based on this concept and carries with it the burden of guilt or the pride of accomplishment. Realizing we're a movement of the larger happening of existence removes us from the karmic wheel of personal responsibility.

It's possible, for those who are interested, to realize we're a movement of existence itself, the same movement that appears as the stars in the night sky or the migration flights of wild birds.

We now appear as we do, but we can just as easily appear to be a pinch of dust or a drop of moisture, and we will at some point; we're a happening without any particular form.

Spiritual awakening is the opening to what actually is, the mystery of it, appearing to be this or that, always moving, shifting, never being anything in particular.

Freedom is being this indefinable vitality, without the strain or effort of needing to be more than that. This doesn't end the pains and difficulties of life; it simply ends the delusion that any of this is being understood or directed.

The various forms appearing in life can't be the reality, because all of them are changing; they're nothing more than false appearances. If we watch a cloud and it takes on the shape of a person, a house, or a mountain, it doesn't matter what it looks like, we always know it's a cloud. The appearance of form is not the reality; the unformed cloud is.

The same is true of everything: bodies, objects, sensations, moods, thoughts, activities, states of mind, relationships, and so on. All apparent things are changing, flowing. They're the passing appearances of a great, unformed, and inexplicable happening — a giant cloud, an event, a presence — call it whatever you have to.

In the same way the appearances of a cloud move to its nature, all appearances move to the nature of existence. We mistake this inexplicable, unformed flow as a collection of things and its impersonal dance as a human accomplishment.

Spiritual awakening can't build an ideal society, because it's the realization that nothing we do is autonomous; our apparent personal actions are the impersonal movement of existence. Everything, just as it is in any apparent moment, is the already complete and pure expression of nature.

Everything we've apparently done, are doing now, and will ever do, is a movement of the cosmos. We are that inexplicable happening spontaneously expressing itself.

To realize this is the freedom the great spiritual teachings point to. It's not the freedom to make ourselves and the world match some fantasy of perfection.

There is this odd notion of nature versus nurture, as though the movement of existence is somehow divided into different parts that influence each other. Many of us wonder how much of what we are is our "natural" expression and how much has been conditioned and distorted by bad parenting or societal education.

We seldom consider that bad parenting, and the workings of society, are also the "natural" expressions of existence. A parent's abilities, or lack of abilities, are just as much an expression of nature as anything else; the same is true of each and every apparent person and action in society.

There is no nature versus nurture. Just as the apparently separate forms of an ocean — the tides, currents, bubbles, ripples, and waves — are actually one movement, so is every apparent thing in existence.

Life isn't moving in any particular direction. Always here and now, it's simply without form, never becoming anything other than what it already is: unformed. Ideas of evolution, direction, and progress are fantasies.

Stories of evolution, direction, and progress apply to the passing appearances of form, but form is a mirage. Any identifiable form, or "thing", that appears to be existing now, is always changing in some way, and will disappear at some point. There is only inexplicable un-form; it's not becoming something else.

Ask three friends to sit around a table with you. Place a cup and a glass on the table. Put the cup closest to you and put the glass on the other side of the cup.

Now say to your friends that you're going to tell them the truth of what's happening on the table, *"The cup is in front of the glass."*

"Wrong," says the friend across from you. *"The glass is in front of the cup."*
"Wrong ," says the friend to your right. *"The cup is to the left of the glass."*
"Wrong," says the friend to your left. *"The cup is to the right of the glass."*

You're all wrong. Life is a many-sided event that can't truly be described, because descriptions are always one-sided.

Added to this is the fact that there is ultimately no form to describe; everything is changing. The essential nature of all things is to remain unformed. Even the sense of existing disappears every night, and then apparently reappears.

Descriptions of form are ultimately false. The happening of existence can't be explained in any true way. Realizing this is not another thought: it's the fading of attachment to thought, the end of belief in description.

In its illusions of form, existence manifests in unique ways at all times. You can't find two identical things: no two snowflakes, no two trees, no two leaves, no two beings.

No two people exhibit the same sensibility. Each may consider the fact that climbing Mount Everest brings a strong possibility of death, and while that frightens one, another finds it exciting and challenging.

My manifestation can't be yours. You must manifest in whatever way life manifests you; you're a unique expression of nature. There's no place for you to get to other than your particular expression and, in each apparent moment, you're already that.

I can only respect and encourage your manifestation. No one can ever say what it actually is and no one can tell you what it should be.

To say that one person is doing it right and another is doing it wrong, is like saying one snowflake is doing it right, while another is doing it wrong. It makes no sense.

Taoist Echoes

Seen from the essential fact of change, all things melt into one seamless flow. An un-form presence, it's nothing in particular. All appearances are portions of this; they are expressions of its energy, its nature.

The only effective remedy for suffering is in acknowledging the unformed nature of all things.

Happiness and sadness come and go regardless of our wishes. We can't hold to one and avoid the other. Now brave, now fearful, now clear, now confused, now happy, now sad; never tied to one road.

The way of life is ingrained; it's not a path to be pointed to; it's not something from which you can deviate. You don't consciously digest the food you eat or make the breath arise and pass. You don't make your blood flow, choose your interests, or create your understandings. Events happen by themselves.

Reflections II

We automatically respond correctly to any situation, since we're capable of responding in only one way, with whatever response nature presents in that moment. There is only what pushes itself to the front in any apparent instant, and all of it is an inexplicable happening.

This realization is not the liberation that most spiritual practitioners are hoping for. They want a story of enlightened beings, and the story of a world moving to a golden age. They want a special self and a special world, instead of awakening from the dream of self and world.

You don't have to learn to let life flow; there is only flow. You don't exist as anything apart from that.

Matter appears to become energy; energy appears
to become matter; liquid appears to become gas; gas
appears to become liquid; heat appears to become
coolness; coolness appears to become heat; and so on.

More precisely, there is no thing called matter
becoming some other thing called energy, any more
than there's some thing called spring becoming some
other thing called summer. These are merely the
passing appearances of a pulsing, surging un-form.

It's like a cloud: one moment it looks like a person
and, in another, it looks like a house. The cloud simply
changes appearance, never becoming anything more
than a cloud. All of existence is this same movement,
appearing to be various things, but never being
anything more than a happening without form.

What's here is here, but what it appears to be is not
what it is. The appearances are constantly altering.
This includes all that you appear to be and all that
you appear to think, say, and do.

Realizing this is not about attaching to another viewpoint; it's about acknowledging a vital, formless dance. The narrow focus on thinking is shifted to the fuller happening of the moment: the totally mysterious, sounding, silencing, lightening, darkening, warming, cooling, pulsing, tingling, trembling event that this moment is.

All sense of directing or understanding this happening evaporates. This isn't some state of mind that we create; it's simply the acknowledgement of what is.

All notions of being something separate from this event disappear. The word "I" is merely a pointer, like the phrase "over there". Whether we look inward, "I", or outward, "over there", all that's found is a vital, pulsing dynamic. With this realization, the word "I" can only point to a vibrant, formless happening; it's not a person with a history.

It's natural for life to present itself as confusion and clarity, anxiety and confidence, sadness and happiness, horror and beauty, and so on. These illusions of form come and go; they're born, they age, and they eventually die, but the unformed liveliness that actually is, is always present, always un-form. It's all that ever is.

We don't have to train ourselves to be part of the flow; everything we appear to be and everything we appear to think, say, and do — all the wonderful stuff and all the ordinary, mundane, unattractive, unhealthy, foolish stuff — is already the divine, mysterious flow. That's all there is.

From a small view it may seem unfair that some get relatively easy lives while others get very difficult situations, but the event that existence is can't be understood as fair or unfair; it's simply a great, mysterious, and often painful, dance.

Spiritual disciplines are not meant to balance the cosmos, nor perfect it. The wholeness that existence is is already balanced in every moment.

It's a simple matter to realize that all of existence is unformed. We can realize that all things in the external world are changing, and, looking inward, we find the same shifting event. Unformed in here; unformed out there; it's one unformed happening. There is no in here or out there; it's one event.

Certain Hindu traditions have the phrase "I am That", signifying the undivided nature of all things. The word universe literally means "undivided turning."

Whether we're astronomers observing galaxies blipping out of existence in the far regions of the universe or we're meditators noticing the disappearing out-breath, all that's ever found is an unformed liveliness.

All things are motion. It's foolishness to label some of it birth and some of it death, because all that ever exists is an ongoing absence of form. How many times in your life have you heard someone say that everything changes? This isn't some strange belief; it's everyone's experience of existence.

In ignoring the vibrant, formless dance that everything actually is, the focus falls on the mirage of form, a "me" and a "world." In general, if it shifts beyond the form of me, it falls on another illusion of form, "us", the human race.

But existence isn't about a me, or an us, or a world. It's an unformed, indefinable happening simply happening.

As long as there's the belief that "we" are separate from, and in control, of this event, there can never be any true compassion. Instead, there is the arrogance of personal accomplishment or failure, a sense of superiority or inferiority.

To realize that all things, including you, are an inexplicable movement spontaneously expressing itself, yields wonder and amazement at all of its apparent manifestations.

Ultimately honouring so-called individuals for their accomplishments, or denouncing them for their failures, is an act of delusion. We're not self-made. No one directs his or her manifestation; no one deserves credit or blame for it.

The morality of humankind is not held in place with preaching. Every society has within it some sense of what the tribe allows and what it does not. This has arisen in the same way language has arisen; it's inherent in the movement of nature.

None of us decided there would be language, and none of us decided there would be a moral sensibility. As our various so-called cultures apparently emerged, a refined sense of morality has emerged.

Each apparent culture, and each apparent individual in that culture, has a different sense of what's right and wrong. Once again, nature manifests in diverse and unique ways.

There are enough similarities, however, to give the mistaken impression that there is a common human morality. As a result, most people consider their own to be the common one and condemn all others. Again there is this arrogance.

There can be no common morality. Each of us exhibits a unique sense of what we can and cannot do, and what we can live with afterwards. The variations may be large and obvious or they may be small and subtle. Fortunately, human beings aren't generally vicious.

This can change in extreme situations of war or deprivation. Various time periods exhibit varying moral standards and a so-called person, at various so-called times, behaves in different ways. Generally the fluctuations aren't large, but they can be.

Reincarnation is a fantasy. Existence has never had a form that could be repeated. The shifting of galaxies on the far side of the universe is the same shifting event of bodies and minds. This happening has no particular form. There is no thing becoming some other thing; there's one great unformed event always remaining unformed.

You don't believe a bear-shaped cloud is really a bear. If the cloud changes shape to look like a horse, you don't believe the bear died and became a horse. You don't actually believe there is a bear or a horse; it's always obviously an unformed happening called a cloud.

You and I are not things becoming other things; we're an unformed happening. Ideas of form don't apply to this. Realization of this is not a matter of describing anything. Realization terminates the strong focus on thoughts and interpretations. Instead, there's a simple acknowledgement of the larger, mysterious dance that this moment is.

Quite obviously, the present moment has no form. Quite obviously, this is the nature of existence.

It's easy to acknowledge that planets are a movement of the universe, and that the earth moves to the rhythms of nature. Landmasses shift; weather changes; plants grow; animals reproduce; bodies develop in other bodies, are delivered, and mature in the biological cycle.

Hearts beat. Breath comes and goes. Blood circulates. Immune systems operate. Seeing, hearing, touching, tasting, smelling, and thinking simply happens. All of this occurs without any effort whatsoever.

Moods shift, ideas alter, perceptions change; it
simply occurs. We are this event — we don't exist as
anything apart from it — yet, somehow, we have the
belief that we're doing it.

Every religion ultimately points to an indefinable
presence that is the ground of all existence. Whether
it's the unfathomable God of the Bible, the enigmatic
asankhata of the Buddhist scriptures, or the
inexplicable, unformed ocean of the Ashtavakra Gita,
the story is the same.

Scientists like Albert Einstein and David Bohm
declare that every so-called thing in existence is
actually an indefinable event.

Science and religion ultimately point to a simple,
observable fact: all of existence is a vital presence that
can't, in any true way, be described. That includes
you.

True humility is realizing this event or presence.
Realizing this destroys the illusion of an independent
will and the arrogance of credit or blame. Judgement

is replaced by wonder and amazement at the infinite variety of nature's appearances, in seeing that each of us is one of those appearances.

If we sit quietly, making no effort, life expresses itself clearly; it simply happens on its own. There's nothing else to get. The great truth is obvious. The heart beats; the breath comes and goes. Vibrations, pulsations, twinges, feelings, thoughts, and emotions rise and fall. Urges rise and pass; some become actions, others do not; and so life flows.

Clarity and confusion, joy and sorrow, hope and despair, and so on, are some of the alternating appearances of that flow.

Even if we try not to move, at some point we're compelled to act. We eat when hungry and sleep when tired. Being the movement of certain pulsations, vibrations, needs, interests, urges, and actions, we automatically function in some way. This process simply happens.

Athletes, artists, intellectuals, parents, politicians, and so on, do not choose their hopes and dreams.

There can be no sense of peace until we realize
we're an indefinable activity. All things, all actions,
all thoughts, words, and deeds, are the passing
appearances and expressions of a great unformed,
indefinable event.

Whose behaviour is free to go in any direction
whatsoever? Each of us must live according to the
physical and mental capacities that nature presents,
centred on the only needs, interests, and concerns
that mysteriously arise in any moment. We don't exist
as anything apart from that.

Realizing this imposes an unshakable humility. Not
the self-absorbed piety of cultivated virtues; instead,
it's the acknowledgement that we can't take credit or
blame for anything. No one can.

We can't judge others for their behaviour; our
apparent doing and their apparent doing is a
movement of the universe according to its physical
makeup. Nothing else is possible.

The average person fears this, imagining this way of
seeing will bring some type of disaster. Perhaps we'll
stop making effort altogether and society will fall

apart. Perhaps we'll become totally irresponsible. After all, if life isn't our doing, it's not our responsibility.

But this is a misunderstanding of what's being said. This is not a situation where you can choose to stop functioning. Instead, it's the realization that your functioning, and non-functioning, have never been your creation.

All of the healthy, responsible, caring behaviour that you've exhibited in life has been the impersonal movement of nature, just as all of the unhealthy, confused, and harmful behaviour has been. There is no you apart from this event.

Seeing this doesn't allow you to leave this process, or lose control of it; there is only this process. Nothing else is evident; nothing else has ever been.

Love and a sense of responsibility are not a personal accomplishment: they're the expression of nature. Everything is. Upon realizing this, respect arises for all of life's manifestations: the horror of some, the enchantment of others, and the wonder of it all.

There's an endless tolerance in knowing that we don't create ourselves. There's compassion in knowing that all of us share this situation.

Life isn't merely a gentle, soothing, experience. Mother Nature is bountiful in her expression, but she also eats her young. In the past, there were symbols that accurately reflected this situation — dark, powerful, mysterious figures like Shiva and Kali.

Nowadays, we seem to emphasize love and peace as the true nature of existence and everything else as some kind of defilement. This isn't a very good preparation for life as it actually is. The full and natural expression of life's dance includes the extremely pleasant and the extremely unpleasant.

The perceiving process searches for patterns and formations in life's flow. This obsessive focus on the mirage of form gives rise to a sense of separation and insecurity. There is the futile hope of finding something stable to cling to: a pleasure, an understanding, a feeling, and so on.

But the search for something stable is endlessly frustrating; there is only flow: unprovoked, unstoppable, ungraspable, and inexplicable.

It's not our failure if life doesn't do what we want, because it's not moving to our command. In any particular moment, life is capable of moving in a direction that isn't wanted and, try as we might, individually and collectively, we can't stop it. We don't exist as anything apart from this flow.

Our bodies, needs, interests, understandings, and abilities are the movement of nature and each expression of nature is unique. If it presents an unusually attractive being from time to time, it's of no relevance to the rest of us.

We can admire someone the way we admire a sunset, but we can't use that person as a model for all of us, anymore than we can pick one sunset and say that all of them should be that.

How much happiness would come from rejecting all expressions of nature except one?

Some teachers declare that we must work to develop morality, wisdom, and the lessening of personal greed. They attract those with a similar attitude. Gathered together, they find it such a pity that others can't see the truth they see, but it's a delusion to think that everyone should be concerned with your particular approach to life.

The nature of existence gives rise to each of our expressions in the same way it sends various birds on their particular migration routes. Even in the case of those that appear to get the same route, they don't occupy the same position in the flock; each is a unique expression.

Whatever you're compelled to be in life, be it, but assuming that everyone should be it is ridiculous. To believe that your way is the only way is like a duck thinking all birds should be ducks.

When a goose flies south in winter, he's not wondering why every other bird isn't following him, and he's not pitying the other birds for not knowing the one true migration route. He doesn't try to convince robins and sparrows to give up their lifestyles for his.

If this so-called enlightenment occurs, it's the simple acknowledgment that every apparent thing in existence is an inexplicable event accomplishing itself.

Looking outward, there's an inexplicable happening; looking inward, there's an inexplicable happening. Unformed there, unformed here, it's an unformed, undivided, indecipherable dance doing what it does.

This so-called awakening is not necessarily pleasant. The impression that existence is being understood and directed melts away, to be replaced with absolute puzzlement.

It's common for childhood views to fall away and be replaced with adult views. In some, the usual adult views will fall away to be replaced with extreme views. In a few others, however, there's the end of belief in any view. The focus of attention is shifted away from thoughts and views, as it becomes obvious that any moment is a larger, inexplicable happening.

This initial shift can be confusing and frightening. All descriptions are invalidated and the sense of free will is eradicated. Even this shift is felt to be occurring independently of what's wanted; it occurs whether it's wanted or not. It's not the result of personal effort; it's the movement of existence itself.

This realization can never be wanted beforehand, because it's the end of all beliefs, hopes, and dreams. It's the end of a describable self. This so-called awakening can never be wanted, but it may happen nonetheless.

This isn't some fleeting mood and it's not the loss of reality; it's the fading away of fantasy. What remains is a mysterious dance spontaneously expressing itself as all apparent things, a magical parade of passing appearances.

Spiritual awakening is often described as the movement into silence, but this can be misleading. It's not a physical silence being described. Instead, the vital, pulsing, sounding event that actually is becomes more evident than ever before.

The silence is the end of attachment to descriptions. The intellectually noisy attachment to frantic thinking, and all of its apparent side effects, is lessened, or silenced, and the larger, enigmatic dance of the moment comes into focus.

There's no struggle to hold it in place, since it has no form. There's no ache to understand it, since it's totally indecipherable. There's no longing for more than what it is, since whatever arises in each moment is all that's possible. There's no oppressive urge to impose any standard, since each expression is unique.

Fears of death no longer make sense; there is only the unfathomable dance of the cosmos. Credit and blame no longer make sense. Pride and shame dissolve and the judging of others becomes impossible.

Obsessive thought, struggle, desire, conformity, fear, pride, shame, and judgement are "silenced" in various ways, and the vital, buzzing event of the moment remains.

Existence expresses itself in shifting appearances: light/dark, sound/silence, warm/cold, joy/sorrow, clarity/confusion, hope/regret, and so on, always shifting from pleasant to unpleasant, back again to pleasant, and repeating. This shifting isn't a failure on anyone's part; it's the essential expression of existence.

This is our reality, always moving to different expressions, forever displaying various appearances viewed as opposites. But they're not opposites: they're the many faces of one dynamic.

Waking up to this essential flow doesn't get rid of it, nor the difficulties of it, but unnecessary struggles and confusions will fall away if it's realized that this is life's natural expression.

The realization that nature expresses itself regardless of our wants can be a frightening proposition, but it's never been any other way.

Seeing this will not promote a slide into disaster. Existence has always expressed both ups and downs — that's its nature — and there's no need to fantasize that it will become entirely negative if this is seen clearly. The wonderful thing about this process is that it generally moves to love. Not the personal love that most people think of; instead, it's an unconditional openness to life.

As we appear to grow older, the fight against life's expression generally fades as the energies of useless opposition grow tired. It's the flowering of all that we are without it needing to be anything else. A difficult aspect of this flowering is its ordinariness. As the grandiose illusions of youth fade, it all seems so mundane, but it's not.

Each of us is an integral and unique appearance of the universe. Everything we appear to be, and all that we appear to think, say, and do, is the automatic and inexplicable dance of the cosmos.

It doesn't matter what part we play, hero or villain, it's a natural expression of existence. Ultimately, as all spiritual teachings indicate, nothing is ever gained or lost. The great, unformed, and inexplicable event that existence is remains unformed and inexplicable.

In old age and death, the melodramatic views of youth recede and the vastness of our situation pushes forward, silencing all objections to it. As we become frail, and wilful energies subside, what has always been becomes obvious: we are life's flow. Even those of us who become delusional will play out our part without any conscious effort.

The fearful urge to keep life under control is based in fantasy. It's the fantasy of thinking oneself separate from the movement of existence, thinking that we direct this movement, and that we had better direct it or it will fall apart.

There's a universal urge to acknowledge a greater power, but the fantasy of a self ruling the world usually takes precedence and is believed to be the truth. Life is an unformed flowing, yet the focus of attention is almost always on illusions of form and the fantasies of people doing things in a world.

If the indecipherable dance of existence is realized, it puts an end to belief in descriptions of me and mine, my life and my doing. That conflicted belief evaporates in a sense of relief and rest.

The idea of spiritual life versus worldly life is a misconception. Everyone is already living the most spiritual life possible, because everything, in any moment, is completely spirit — the spontaneous, unformed, inexplicable swirl that everything actually is.

Human arrogance is the feeling that we're superior to everything else in the cosmos, and that some of us are more highly developed than others of our kind. We either take credit for our superiority, while passing judgement on the shortcomings of others, or, if we're one of the so-called inferior, we take the blame for not being much of anything at all.

This is an interesting view, since everything else in existence — the sun, the moon, the clouds, the seasons, the weather, the animals, and so on — are seen to be the varied and fascinating expressions of nature, none superior to another.

A bird or a planet is not seen to be directing its particular development; everything is generally considered to be an expression of the mysterious dance that existence is. Everything — except for one thing — us. Somehow, there's the belief that we're directing the dance.

This must mean we exist somewhere outside of it. The idea that our bodies, abilities, and actions occur somewhere outside the flow of nature is very strange. Where and how are we existing, if not as part of nature's expression?

We can't truly say what this event of existence is. Even the sense of existing disappears every night, only to reappear. It's like a light blinking off and on.

When it's on, our so-called life appears in its flow. Bodies, needs, interests, concerns, urges, and actions — family situations, national events, international events — all of these arise and fade as passing appearances of a formless event.

There may be hope that life will move in a certain way, but hope doesn't create the potential for that movement. Maybe the potential exists; maybe it doesn't. Life isn't a wilful act; it's a mysterious happening, unpredictably expressing itself.

You wouldn't go to a tropical island paradise just to sit in a hotel reading the brochures that describe the sun, the sand, and the surf. In that situation, it's very easy to see that those descriptions do not contain the fullness, vibrancy, and joy of the actual event called an island paradise, and we would never be content to simply sit in the hotel reading.

Yet most of us do this with life in general, being obsessively focused on the stories of thought, the "brochures" of the mind. Spiritual awakening realizes the ultimate emptiness of description. Instead, there's an interest in life itself, the unformed, inexplicable, vibrant, dancing fullness that this moment actually is.

It's incorrect to describe existence as individuals influencing life or as life influencing individuals. The perceptual process mistakenly views the formless flow of existence as separate forms influencing each other, or as a journey from one phase to another. It even mistakenly thinks there's a perceptual process.

I'm not telling anyone to "go with the flow", because there is only flow. I'm not saying "bring yourself into alignment with the movement of life", because there is only movement; there is no you apart from it.

There's no possible way for you to be out of alignment with the flow of existence; there is only that.

Shades of Advaita

We are the unformed flow of existence itself; we're already and eternally that.

You don't need to acquire anything new, just give up false ideas. Outside the fantasies of thought, there are no entities called self and world. There is no creation or destruction, free will or destiny, ignorance or enlightenment. There is no wandering in the wilderness and coming to the light.

Our real nature is liberation. We are the unconstrained dance of the cosmos itself. We imagine we're bound as separate individuals and make strenuous efforts to be free, when all the while we're already free.

We ignore the unformed, inexplicable dance that life is and imagine forms of body and mind to be reality. It's this mistaken belief in form that gives rise to misery.

Reflections III

Our apparent needs, interests, and concerns come together as an apparent thirst. It may be the thirst for love, understanding, adventure, money, power, knowledge, family, and so on. It may be one or more of these.

This thirst will adjust itself from moment to moment. It may be as simple and direct as needing a meal or wanting entertainment, or it may be as complex, and long term, as needing children or wanting to understand existence. Whatever it is, in any moment, it pushes itself forward, setting all priorities.

Realizing that everything is the impersonal flow of nature doesn't make every moment clear and pleasant; it's just as much the expression of nature to be vague and unpleasant.

The ordinary human mind, in any moment, with all of its apparent confusions, sorrows, and wants, is already the complete and natural expression of the Divine, the Unformed, the Tao, Buddha Mind, God, Brahma, and so on. These are the various labels for the inexplicable happening that everything is.

When it's realized that every thought, word, and deed is the natural expression of existence then you're free to move without the conflict of feeling defective or incompetent. The dance of existence isn't defective or incompetent in any way.

Spiritual liberation frees you from the misery-inducing fantasy of perfecting yourself. In this moment, I am what I am; you are what you are; we're both the dance of the cosmos. Liberation isn't the act of breaking free of this. Liberation is knowing it can't be otherwise.

Just as a growing plant contains all the direction it needs to be the plant that it is, we contain all the direction we need to be the person that we are.

Everything in existence has an innate intelligence, an essential current expressing itself. Whatever you are, in any moment, is the expression of that current. There is only that current, or flow; that's what everything is.

An ocean doesn't direct its own movement; it doesn't need to struggle to express its true nature. In each moment, it's all that it can possibly be; each wave, ripple, and swirl is fine.

Fantasized notions of perfection and standards of conformity are a denial of life's flow, a denial of life's expression. Stories of individuals falling from purity to defilement are a fantasy. Nothing has fallen anywhere; everything is always the complete and natural expression of existence or, if you prefer, the expression of God.

Your fullness is whatever arises in any particular moment. This can't be classified as spiritual or worldly; it can't be classified as right or wrong: there's no way of saying what any of this actually is.

The general statement that life is about spiritual awakening, or the development of wisdom and compassion, is incorrect. That statement is merely the propaganda of groups primarily focused on spiritual matters.

Life exhibits no observable goal other than expressing itself in diverse and unique ways. For every apparent person primarily focused on wisdom and compassion, there are many who aren't. It's not that they've failed to realize a truth; they're simply a different expression of existence, an expression that's just as valid as any other.

If you're practising forgiveness, forgiving others for their behaviour, be aware that you're primarily practising judgement and blame. Before you can forgive someone you must first make them guilty of an offence.

This is a denial of life. Our urges and actions are expressions of nature; no one can be blamed for being the particular arrangement of abilities, urges, and actions they are.

Some expressions of existence are naturally considered to be unpleasant, or even dangerous, and we will respond automatically to that unpleasantness or danger. However, just as a volcano doesn't need to be forgiven for its unpleasant, or dangerous, behaviour, neither does any person.

There is the notion that all awakened beings will behave in the same way, matching some societal fantasy of what a saint should be. In actuality, they come in all sizes, shapes, and temperaments; some are not pleasant.

They all see themselves as the inexplicable dance of existence, but this doesn't make them conform to some fantasy of perfection. It doesn't even necessarily make them sociable.

Truth, reality, God — however you want to label it — is a vital presence, a dynamic event. It's not a particular object, idea, feeling, mood, and so on. It's the inexplicable flow of existence and we've never been anything apart from that.

Existence can be summed up in one short Zen verse:

Sitting quietly,
doing nothing,
spring comes,
grass grows by itself.

The same is true of everything: the ageing of the body, the movement of thoughts and moods, urges to action, and actions themselves. Everything simply happens, like spring coming and grass growing.

Sitting quietly, you'll find that whatever you are, in any particular moment, presents itself automatically. Needs, interests, and concerns push themselves to the front and play out in whatever way they do.

In certain times, it's light and calm; in others, dark and stormy. In each moment, it's a totally mysterious event doing what it does.

Sitting quietly, making no effort, all is revealed: a vibrant, pulsing, formless happening, simply happening. There is no goal in this, no final point; there is only what expresses itself in this moment, and whatever it appears to be now is unavoidably on its way to some other appearance.

One of the delusions of ego is that it operates outside of the flow of cause and effect and that it's able to influence that stream by introducing something new to it. But it's never been anything separate from that flow, something that could inject anything new.

Improvements appear to occur, just as downturns do, but these are the rhythmic expressions of nature, the waves of a mighty ocean; it's not anyone's personal achievement or failure.

Anyone who appears to produce something of benefit to themselves, or to the world at large, is compelled to do so. The fascination with a particular subject, an urge to explore, an intuition, a thought, an ability, or a fortunate accident, is never anyone's personal creation.

When Einstein was complimented on his discovery of the theory of relativity, he would say it simply happened, that he didn't make it happen.

There are myriad stories of scientists investigating various subjects and, in a moment when they were relaxing or sleeping, making no effort whatsoever — not even focusing on their interest — some great discovery popped up in a thought, a vision, or a dream.

This is not a matter of "discovery"; this is simply the inexplicable dance of existence expressing itself.

We can't have up without down, joy without sorrow, confidence without anxiety, and so on. These are the natural expressions of life. If existence appears to move one way now, it will move in the apparently opposite direction at some point. This has nothing to do with anyone's efforts; this is the natural rhythm of existence.

There's nothing we can do to change this. Even if we live in the wisest way possible, existence will continue to express itself in this manner. Life is always a unique blend of apparent opposites and there's no "me" that gets to choose the mix.

The waxing and waning of emotions and states of mind are like the flowing of the seasons. We may anticipate them and prepare for them, but we can't prevent them. We don't exist as anything apart from that flow.

If I say to you there is no me, no you, no self, no world, no thinking, no personal actions, no forms of any kind, I'm not talking about some experience that's different from yours.

This is not describing some altered state; I'm pointing to the basic happening that you are right now; it's simply being acknowledged precisely.

Spiritual awakening or enlightenment doesn't add anything more to what's existing. Instead, it's the fading away of fantasies. What then remains is what has been here all along, an inexplicable dance.

When I say that's what remains, don't get the idea of some strange experience without thought. What is usually called a me, a you, a self, and a world, including thought -that still happens — but there's no longer any obsessive belief in those false forms and labels. Instead, the absolutely inexplicable movement, or unformed flowing, that everything is becomes obvious.

Question and Answer: Part II

Q: I want to ask you about the basic qualities that are said to arise with spiritual awakening, such as compassion, detachment, and harmony. You've touched on some of these already, but I want to take more time with them.

I thought we could start with a consideration of compassion. Within most spiritual circles, the theme of compassion is very strong. We're urged to cultivate it and it's often coupled with wisdom as the ultimate expression of existence.

DB: Yes, people in spiritual circles often believe that wisdom and compassion are the goals of existence. They fantasize that an awakened being becomes some extraordinary fountain of love, giving endlessly to the greater good of humankind. They tend to ignore the stories of enlightened beings who, upon awakening, left society to live on their own.

Awakened beings don't gain the power to throw off their personalities; they continue to be expressions of nature. It's ironic that people have preconceived notions of what an enlightened personality is, or how that personality will behave, because each expression of nature is unique.

Some teach; some don't. Some talk; some don't. Some enjoy society; some don't. Some are pleasant personalities; some not. Some are married; some single. Some sexual; some celibate. Some live in a traditional religious environment; others do not. Some sit quietly for long periods; others don't. Some seem to make sense; others seem to be crazy. And so on.

What they have in common is the absolute certainty that everything is an unformed, inexplicable happening presenting itself.

Realizing this mysterious dance gives rise to a natural tolerance for all of life's expressions. Not only a tolerance, but the acknowledgment and appreciation that everyone is a unique expression and has to be that particular expression.

This is the compassion of awakening. It doesn't

necessarily mean we like all things, or endlessly serve others, but we can appreciate that everything must be whatever it is in any particular moment.

Some awakened beings appear to serve in extraordinary ways; others appear to be nothing more than mildly good-natured; some may even appear be grouchy and intolerant. No one knows what any of this actually is and anyone who says they do is deluded.

Q: *What about harmony? How does harmony arise?*

DB: Harmony is contentment with life as it is, with all of its inevitable expressions. Seeing that everything is an expression of the cosmos, there's no longer the desire for anything more than what it offers.

Q: *How do we know what it offers?*

DB: Whatever happens is what it offers. There's never any mistake, because all of life is the impersonal expression of nature.

Q: *And seeing this is detachment?*

DB: Yes. It eventually doesn't matter what thought wants, because the various expressions of nature don't move to the wishes of thought; thought is simply one of the various expressions. Anything that appears to arise is unavoidably on its way to another expression, so why get attached to any of it?

This is not saying that with detachment there will never be desire, sorrow, confusion, anxiety, and so on. It's not saying that you won't participate in society. Life will continue to express whatever it expresses, but there's no extended concern over anything that happens. All of it is felt to be the complete and natural movement of existence. That's detachment.

Q: *What about love? In the Advaita tradition, one often hears old masters saying things like,* "You are not the body; you are not the mind; there is only love."

DB: Yes, that's the traditional expression; Robert Adams used to say it all the time. Love, in its highest philosophical sense, is an openness to all that life offers.

Everything, just as it is in any particular moment, is the complete and natural expression of existence moving to its inherent nature. Love is the simple acknowledgement of that.

Profound spiritual teachings are not prescriptions for perfecting life. They simply point to the already complete and pure expression of existence. There's the realization that everything is happening the only way it can. Realizing this brings a sense of contentment to life, with all of its apparent joys, sorrows, conflicts, and brutalities.

Again, be careful with this. It's not saying that you'll sit around doing nothing and never oppose or pursue anything; it's simply saying that whatever happens, in any apparent moment, is the unavoidable expression of existence. Nothing else is possible.

In spiritual circles we're often urged to move deep within ourselves to find a place of peace, but this is misleading. The place of our life is always the fullness of the present moment. Awakening isn't about moving to a different place; it's about a different sense of the same place.

As long as there's the fantasy that you're directing existence, life will never be enough. With the realization that everything is a movement of the cosmos, an underlying sense of peace, well-being, and openness is present in some variation, no matter what happens, because all of it is felt to be the natural dance of existence.

That peace, well-being, and openness is often called love.

Q: *How does humility arise?*

DB: What could be more humbling than to discover you're not personally responsible for anything you think, say, and do? You can no longer praise yourself for positive things; they can only be appreciated. You can no longer wallow in self-pity or recrimination for any so-called negative things; they can only be lived out.

The belief in personal doing is replaced with the simple acknowledgment of life's mysterious dance. This is not some cold, sterile, situation; it's exactly the same event that is usually perceived as people in a world. The labels and stories still arise as part of the flow, but there's no sense of understanding any of it; it simply happens, a vibrantly rich and magical parade of appearances.

Q: *When all is said and done, where does this leave us?*

DB: We continue to be whatever nature expresses in any particular moment. The ignorant assumption that it could ever be otherwise comes to an end.

Life will not express itself in a continuously calm and clear fashion. In certain periods, there can be stomach-twisting, head-pounding energies pushing and pulling in many directions, with no indication of how it will all play out.

The natural current of life is showing itself just as much in periods of intense vagueness and confusion as it is in periods of certainty and clarity.

The average so-called person isn't comfortable as the process they are. Most of us feel inadequate, or inferior, to others who appear to be more competent and happy. The most judgemental human beings are often the students of spiritual teachings. Not because they intentionally want to judge others, but because they carry the fantasy of a perfect being and hope to become that.

This hopeful fantasy doesn't allow for periods of

confusion, anger, jealousy, fear, aggression, and so on. Many people view those expressions as being tainted and distorted in some way and will fall into periods of self-loathing for exhibiting this natural human behaviour.

Can you imagine a robin covering its face with its wing as it breaks down, sobbing, *"I can't believe I chirp and eat worms. Why, why, why can't I get rid of this behaviour?"* You laugh, but is it any different from a meditator sobbing, *"Why do I still get angry, jealous, fearful, and confused?"*

How many of us have prepared ourselves to act in a reasonable, calm manner when anticipating an upcoming stressful situation, but, when the moment actually arrives, we find ourselves emotionally unhinged?

This isn't our personal failure; it's the fact that our will is not ruling existence. We're a movement of nature and, no matter what the mind wishes, we have to be whatever nature expresses in any particular moment.

If there's a profound realization of this, there can be

moments of absolute clarity regarding the truth of it, the feeling that there is nowhere else to get to, and nothing else to be, other than whatever presents itself in each instant. All of it is a fascinating and totally inexplicable event presenting itself.

Initially, even with deep realization, this clarity can alternate with the old illusion of being someone separate from the world, a someone desperately needing understanding and control.

At first, there will be the desire for this fluctuation to end, leaving only the feeling of clarity, but as it becomes obvious that this fluctuation is also life's natural expression, it ceases to be worrisome. At times, existence may literally feel like one great ocean moving and shifting and, at other times, that universal sense may be barely noticeable. Eventually, though, the idea that life is our doing comes to an end.

Right now, my favourite spiritual story is one of a Zen master who's dying and his students have gathered to witness his passing.

Zen masters have a reputation for uttering something profound just before they expire. There was one who, upon hearing a squirrel running across the roof tiles, sat up proclaiming, *"Just this; nothing more"*, before falling back dead. Others have uttered marvellous poems on the links between human life and nature's flow. Consequently, these particular students are waiting in great anticipation for the final moments.

The master is having trouble speaking, so he's given paper and brush to enable him to make a statement. He writes something, hands the paper back, and the students read, *"I don't want to die."*

Surprised by this, since it seems to express desire, and believing that Zen masters are beyond such human traits, the students immediately assume it must have a deeper meaning. They again give the master paper and brush, begging him to explain the real meaning of his words. Once more the old man writes something and gives the paper back. This time the students read, *"I really, really, don't want to die."*

The point is this: the master is free to be whatever he is, without apology or regret. The students, however, live in fantasies of what life should be; they're unable to acknowledge the simple facts of the moment, the simple expression of existence.

In this moment, you may love your life or you may hate it. You may be confused and frightened or clear and calm. You may be on a spiritual path or a course of crime. You may be a worldly success or a failure. You may be living to feed the poor or living only to acquire money. You may be anything a human being can appear to be and not for one moment have you stopped being the complete and pure expression of existence.

Q: *That seems like the perfect note to end on. Thank you for taking the time and trouble to do this.*

DB: I'm not doing this, and you're welcome.

Nothing ever comes to stay, to "be".
There is no "being", only endless becoming.

But there's never any real becoming.
Nothing comes to stay, to "be".

Nothing ever "is",
There is no "isness", only change, or movement.

But there's never any real change or movement.
There's never any "thing" to change, to move.

There's simply the absence of form.
Movement is the ongoing absence of form.

But there's never any real absence of form.
Form has never existed. How could it possibly be absent?

Nothing is ever established or defined. There is no
arriving. There is no being, no "isness", no becoming.
No thing, no change, no movement.
No presence and no absence.

Just this.

Just this.

Life's struggle
is just
a lack of light,
the sense of rush
and endless flight,
a ripple's vain
and angst-filled fight
to find its way
back to an
ever-shifting sea,
when all the while
nothing else
exists.

There is no you;
there is no me;
and yet
it is so
nice
to dream
so,
until a moment's
sanity
erodes that long
held fallacy,
and leaves
just one
great truth-filled
pulse.

Mind comes before
all things.
What kind of foolishness
is that?
Illusion comes before
a mind;
that has always been
the fact.
All form is truly
without form,
and mind,
another form along
the way.
It's just a
misconception,
an ocean,
now,
at play.

A great ocean,
whose tides
and rivers
appear
as
things,
gives birth
to newborn
babes,
and the
river's way
is written
in their new
and pudgy
flesh.

I think
of words
to paint life's
mighty sea,
but they are never
as splendid
as the real
thing.
For oceans are
a vital dance,
beyond the mind's
caprice,
and live a life
of liberty
outside of
thought's
convention.

They never stop,
these pains of change.
Internal surging,
exquisite bursting
seams
of present comfort.
Moving now,
receding,
then driving forth again.
Ever pulsing,
never arriving.
Life.

What greater law to serve
than life's determined
flow?
What greater will
to follow
than the manifesting
now?
What greater love
to live
than the present
sweet, sweet
storm?

Life's ocean
never
changes:
heave
and roll,
in fine-spun
mist,
conception.

This
movement
round the unfold
enfolds
twice times more
than we
can
imagine
and left agog
is truly
awe,
enticing only
yes.
For what else
can be done?

And all
the struggles
cease.

Endnotes

This book is primarily composed of fragments from conversations with various people over many years.

Taoist Echoes and *Shades of Advaita*, were prompted by the teachings of the Taoist masters, Lao Tzu, Chuang Tzu, and Lieh Tzu, and the twentieth century Advaita master, Ramana Maharshi, as presented in the works of Timothy Freke and David Godman respectively. *"Echoes"* and *"Shades"* were originally much longer pieces for my own enjoyment. They're not a collection of exact quotations, but carry the essential message of the original texts.

Advaita is an ancient teaching of India; so is Buddhism. Taoism is an early teaching of China. Chan (Zen) also began in China, and is basically Buddhism mixed with Taoism.

About the Author

Spontaneously drawn to meditation at age fourteen, Darryl spent the next seventeen years exploring the awareness and concentration teachings of Buddhism, Taoism, Sufism, Hinduism, Christianity, and Western psychology. He then spent nine years apprenticed to mindfulness teacher Ruth Denison and another six years as a meditation monk in the Thai Forest Tradition of Theravada Buddhism, under the guidance of Ajahn Sumedho.

Along the way, there was recurring contact with the independent philosopher, Jiddu Krishnamurti, and a significant connection with the Advaita sage, Robert Adams.

Darryl has worked as an ice fisherman, bus driver, suit salesman, carpenter, child-care worker, and maintenance man, among other things. He has lived, and taught, in England, Switzerland, and the United States. He currently lives, works, and teaches in Winnipeg, Canada.

Acknowledgments and Appreciation

To my mother, Gwen, my father, Ed, and my brother, Brent, for their love and unconditional acceptance.

To Jiddu Krishnamurti, Ruth Denison, Ajahn Sumedho, and Robert Adams, for their presence in my life and all that they offered.

To Alan Watts, Ramesh Balsekar, and U.G. Krishnamurti, for their recorded words.

To Sandra Stuart and Link Phillips, for their companionship and talent in the birthing of two books and the remodelling of another. It was in conversations with Sandra that I first expressed my views openly and she subsequently offered the encouragement and opportunity for sharing them with a larger audience.

Again to Sandra and Link, as well as to Valerie Metcalfe and Sally Perchaluk, for their reflections on the rough draft of this present work.

To Wendy Rondeau for offering my books to Joan Tollifson. To Joan for her strong acknowledgment and the referral to Julian Noyce. To Julian, for his efforts over the years in publishing expressions of perennial truths, as well as his willingness to publish radically different expressions.

To Mary Wall, Nick Herzmark, Keith Millan, Dianne Wilt, Anna Millan, Toan Tran, Dale Purvis, Jon Mousely, Jill Osler, Karen Clements, Brenda Reimer-Dorratt, Juliette Sabot, Dale Ingram, Sheila Konyk, Ruth Wood, and Norma Nickson for their support in various ways.

And to many others, too numerous to mention.

If you enjoyed this book, you might be interested in these related titles published by Non-Duality Press.

Books for 2011
from
Non-Duality Press

The Ultimate Twist *by* Suzanne Foxton
A non-dual novella

The Almighty Mackerel and His Holy Bootstraps
by JC Amberchele

The Telling Stones *by* Riktam Barry
Enlightenment, the 1960's and modern times

Goner *by* Louis Brawley
The Final Travels of UG Krishnamurti

The Loving Awareness in Which All Arises
by Rick Linchitz
Dialogues on awakening

Blessed Disillusionment *by* Morgan Caraway
Seeing Through Ideas of Self

The Last Hustle *by* Kenny Johnson
Finding true happiness and freedom in prison

CPSIA information can be obtained
at www.ICGtesting.com
Printed in the USA
LVOW08s1540200517
535244LV00001B/23/P